Midnight Scribbles

Maddison Hayward

BookLeaf Publishing

India | USA | UK

DEDICATION

For Dan, love of my life, and the only person who acts impressed by my scribbles.

ACKNOWLEDGEMENT

Author photograph by Jason Murray
Cover photo by Rachel Gilroy
Cover designed by Shanelle Forbes

PREFACE

"Poetry is an amazing way to unscramble the things in our heads and hearts. It's like a silent therapist that we can share things with..."
-A Very Wise Woman

Fight

Bury your pain
Deep down, in the ground.
Silence your scream
Not a peep, not a sound.

Smile all day
Smile at them, smile at me.
Don't let us see
Who you are, who you'll be.

Dig down within
In your heart, in your soul
Find something more
Take hold, take control.

Stand strong and tall
Don't sleep, get on your feet.
Your life is your war
Never die, never defeat.

Don't say it's too late
Start the fight, hide the hurt.
Eyes up and fists raised
Bite your lip, taste the dirt.

Hold on and you'll know
Just like them, just like me.
Pain won't take you down.
You are brave. You are free.

Claustrophobic

I feel cramped in a place that could hold half the
sea
Because space without you seems to smother
me.
There's nothing to talk about, no one to call.
Without you my world is too small.
Nowhere to go and nothing to see
With no you there's only me.
Now my life is small and empty

Feeling lost and it's all going wrong
Like I lost the lyrics of my favourite song.
The walls are closing in- I'm claustrophobic.
Can't hear the music, only feel the clock tick.
When you leave you take everything with you
So why didn't you just take my heart too?

So full of nothing I can't even feel.
My world so small, every dream feels real.
Nothing to do now, nowhere to go.
If I did something, no one to show.
When you go you leave nothing behind
Took my life and left nothing but time.

Too much, too little, wasting my time.

If you're not here can't call you mine.
Running in circles but try not to care.
Silent, I'm hiding and I can't breathe air.
Who knew the universe could be so small?
Because without you there's nothing at all.

Now I feel cramped in a place that could hold hold
half the sea
Because space without you seems to smother
me.
There's nothing to talk about, no one to call.
Without you my world is too small.
Nowhere to go and nothing to see
With no you there's only me
Now my life is small and empty.

Invisible

Behind my eyes you cannot see
A thousand ways I've died.
Take a pin and prick my skin,
You cannot see inside.
The lives I've lived
The scars that give
A story to my soul.
When you look at me
All you will see
Is a life that's still untold.

Hear a whisper, take a peak
At a life you'll never know.
And deep within my buried sin
Rips my heart to and fro.
When demons wake
And strong minds break
You still won't see a thing.
Because when you look at me
All you can see
Is a smile thrown to the wind.

Free

Look into my eyes
Look into nothing
Look at where I am
A world of endless despair.

Without compassion
Without a glance
Without an effort
You spilt my life on the floor.

Your bed of beautiful lies
Your twisted tongue
Your forgotten promises
My eternal ruin.

Taught me empty love
Taught me trust is pain
Taught me to be silent
To hide my life away.

Left me without feeling
Left me without meaning
Left me without light
But I feel better in the dark.

Inside I keep my feeling
Inside I search for meaning
Inside I am still living
You can't take what you can't see.

I never want to love again
I won't give in to trust
I have become what you wanted
You won, but I won't be your prize.

Keep the shreds of my happiness
Keep my broken, shattered heart
Keep everything you took from me
I am incomplete but free.

Dream

Come with me to a land my own
A place I go to escape from home.
Stay where you are and close your eyes
Now dream up your own sweet lies.

Imagination gives you wings
To other places and better things.
Don't restrain it, set it free
Let it decide your destiny.

No rules, no limits, everything to find
You are your own world's mastermind.
Travel, romance, riches, and fame,
Wonders only fancy can claim.

Now come back with a jarring thud
Back to earth, with mental flood.
Dreams are sweet, dreams are free
But never change reality...

Past VS Future

Winter has come
Dawn of a cold night
The moon warms my face
Shadows dance in the light.

Is it a dream?
All that I loved calls
An invitation to eternal past
Whispered promises, soft footfalls.

Inside I know
I could find a release
Living in broken hopes and dreams
In the corpse of my past find peace.

An ethereal promise
Of delight so tempting
Past loves beckon
Memories teasing and taunting.

But holding me back
In persistent restraint
A memory distant
Pleading, but faint.

From the future
A voice I once knew
Begging me to stay
In a life empty but true.

A love forgotten
Returns from unknown
Somewhere in my future
I'll no longer be alone.

Back from the edge
Away from the past turn
Your love of the future
I must stay and learn.

Travelling on
In moonlight's brilliance
Voices from my past
Fade in the distance.

On you lead
Like a secret dance
For the promise of love
I'll give the future a chance.

The Stranger

I stare at the mirror and what do I see?
The face of a stranger looking back at me.
I wonder about the person there
With my nose and long brown hair.
Strangely alike, but so far apart.
How could we possibly share the same heart?
In my minds eye I'm clearly depicted
As a beautiful girl, not at all hieght restricted.
And should you ask me I would describe
Myself as not being half so wide!
That stranger in the looking glass
Doesnt posses half my class!
My own eyes contain laughter and fun.
So different from this lonely looking one.
Though the hint of a hidden smile is there
It's hidden by pain, sorrow and care.
Surely we're not at all the same
The figure in the mirror is some kind of game!
I know that the glass is supposed to show
Just me and no one else, although
I think right now it's telling a lie.
If that's really me I'd rather die!
I have come to the relieving conviction
That the stranger I see is completely fiction.
Where she came from and why she's there

I dont know, and why should I care?
As long as I know that she isnt me
For a sorrier creature I never did see.
But what if we stripped off all the skin
And took a look at our hearts within?
Would I find the same hopes and dreams?
The same strong will pushing to the extremes?
Strangely enough that's just what I find.
How could a stranger know my own mind?
It seems that I have made a mistake.
The girl in the mirror really isnt a fake.
Now when I look in the mirror I know what I see
For that stranger there really is me!

The Black Princess

Alone in this tower far away
I pace cold halls and cry.
Never do I see the light of day
For the Black Princess am I.

Here in my dark world of pain,
Locked in this castle of despair,
I try to escape, but alas, in vain,
I trip over things that aren't there.

Always I have reigned here on my own.
Black Princess of the land of night.
Fear and Pain, they share my throne,
While nightmares on my shoulders alight.

Whispering in my ear they tell me
It shall always be this way.
Wrapped in black shroud of misery
Here in the dark I will stay.

My tears are black of ebony
Ever dripping of my face.
Unseen fingers of ice hold me,
Dragging me to a lower place.

Eerie shadows dance on the wall
As I wander the empty corridor
Screaming out but none here my call,
Only the bones of those gone before.

I look into an empty sky
Searching for dawn of endless night.
As I scan something catches my eye-
A twinkling pinpoint of light.

As I watch slowly it grows
Until it fills the whole sky.
Everything round me starts to glow
Reflecting the star from on high.

No longer I be the Black Princess
For the black now reflects another hue.
Under the star's gentle caress
Violet my world does renew.

The Violet Princess now am I.
Hope lives, fear runs in dread.
Black tears no more I cry,
But sweetly smile instead

I Want

I want to be pretty.
I want to be smart.
I want to be kind,
To have a good heart.

But I'm not pretty,
And I'm not smart.
I try to be kind,
But I fail before I start.

I make more mistakes
Than those around me.
They must think I'm cruel
But if only they could see...

Because on the inside
I'm trying to do right
Make others happy
Share smiles bright.

But always I fall
Right down to my knees.
Could someone tell me
Whats wrong with me please?

For all my intentions
No matter how great they be
Never seem to go right...
Just hurting those I see.

Let me say sorry
For all the things I've done
I never wanted to hurt you
No, not anyone.

I'm going to try harder
To show love to all
Do acts of kindness
No matter how small.

Maybe pretty
I'll be thought of this way
It's the inside that counts
To God anyway.

Wisdom I will have
Though smart I may not be
What good are report cards
When it comes to 'Eternally'?

God, grant me wisdom,
And a beauty inside.
Give me a light

That I just cant hide.

Make me a tower
Of strength for my friends.
Give me humility
So I can make amends.

Let me then beg you
To let me try again.
I know I've failed you
Been the worst kind of friend.

Please remember
that I love you all
I want to be here for you
Whenever you fall.

I want to share
Your smiles and tears
I want to be your friend
Down through the years

The Drive To Go

Here we go again, no change in you
No giving credit where it's due.
You always have to put me down
Say I'll never be better than you.
Should we just take your word?
You haven't proved a thing.
You're scared of effort and of scars
So you'll never reach for the stars.

I never thought you'd be this way
But I heard from you the other day.
You cheat and lie but you're afraid.
So now this is what I have to say
I'm not afraid to take a stand
While all you do is sit.
Don't preach what you won't walk
'Cause I'm sick of nothing but talk.

Just because you don't believe in me
Doesn't mean that I can't be.
Your negativity won't hold me back
All my hopes and dreams I'll achieve.
I can do more than you thought I could
Don't try and bring me down
You will never stand where I stood

And you're never going to feel this good.

Stick this in your pipe and smoke it
I'm going to be all you ever wanted.
You think you're better than everything I've got
But I'll prove you wrong when I make it to the
top.
You may have the skill but they'll never know.
I've got something you've never shown.
Baby, it takes the drive to go.

You know that I'm too good for you.
In fact, I'm moving right along.
My dreams and sweat have pulled me through
Now you're just a lyric to my song.

Fly

Take me far away from here,
My world of hate and fear
To a place where I can rest,
A place of love and cheer.

I fall further every day.
The scars, they do not fade away
Life drains freely from my veins
Staining all I do and say.

Away from this I want to fly
On wings of light, way up high.
Sweeping, soaring, wild and free,
Never come back, never die.

My Star

Once I caught a starlight beam
Its beauty beyond compare.
I loved my star with all my heart
But one day it wasn't there.

I had bid my star to run away
Love to it I would no more give.
I had been dazzled by the sun
Under its light I wanted to live.

I told my star I loved it not
But my heart I did deceive.
My star left sadly, quietly,
Though my lie it did not believe.

For a time I bore the sun's rays
Glaring, hot, and strong.
I missed my star's gentle light
And knew I had been wrong.

To the sun I had been drawn
For many more lived there.
But here I found I didn't belong-
My star and I were a pair.

Joyful in my discovery
I went in search of my star
Only to find I was too late.
My star had traversed too far.

Claimed again and out of reach.
My star no longer my own.
Why did I ever let it go?
I had lost my one true home.

Heartbroken and knowing
There was only me to blame,
I turned around, tried to let go
And to forget my star's name.

But the Ruler of the Heavens
Had decided we were to be.
My star and I crossed paths again
With happiness and painful memory.

Looking into each other's eyes
Love so strong we could see.
Never again could we say goodbye
To the others heart we held the key.

It took some time and hurt
Before my star could again be mine
Forgiveness had to take place
And trust rebuilt over time.

Stronger are we for the parting
Now nothing our love could break.
My star forever will be my own.
Nothing else my love ever take.

Run Away With Me

I see the tears running down your cheek,
The look in your eyes, more empty each week.
Trapped in a graveyard of broken dreams
Kisses of ice and silent screams.
It's not enough to leave you here
In dreams of poison and lies of fear.

Let go, break free, run away with me.

The world gives you nothing to hold onto,
Feel like you'll drown no matter what you do.
Looking for something but nowhere to look
Ripping wasted pages from your life's book.
You don't belong here, nor do I.
Let's run away and stop this lie.

Hold on, break free, run away with me.

In the end it's all going to be the same
Just a big question of loss or gain.
Don't know where we're going, don't understand
But take the chance and take my hand.
No looking back, no looking down
Jump now and hear the silence of sound.

Stay close, break free, run away with me.

And where we are no feet the the ground,
Heightened senses of taste, touch, and sound.
Give me your heart and I'll give you mine
In this place where we left our lives behind.

Here we go, we're free, run away with me.

My Ghost

You're somewhere just beyond me
I can feel you under my skin.
Like my breathe of life I can't see you
Like the pain in my chest, I feel you.
You're constantly watching
But you're never there.
An illusion floating through my dreams
As real as the tears everywhere.
I quiver under your touch in my sleep
I long for yours arms in my day.
I've met you in a vision,
But I can't make out your face.
You are the answer to my emptiness
The heart to give me a place.
Until I find you my life is waiting.
And I am longing
For you mystery to fade away.
You may never come to me
But I'll search til my dying day.

Antidote of Love

I don't know why I'm feeling
Thought my heart had died
But here I am- I need you
And you're healing me inside.

Don't know if I like it
Confusion starts to rise.
Trying to read the future
Every time I see your eyes.

Betrayal and disappointment
Froze my heart so long ago.
But now your smile melts me
And I really want to know

Are you going to hurt me
Or help me learn to feel?
Show me love and trust
So I know they are real?

A poison of uncertainty
Won't let me be yours
A name that's been forgotten
My heart behind locked doors.

Kiss me like I'm dying
And the antidote's your tongue.
Call my name out strongly
Like a song that needs to be sung.

Help me fall in love for real
I only want it to be you.
Don't let me break my heart again
Show me our feelings are true.

Life

Life is but a vapour
Nothing in it, nothing to it
Its enjoyments empty bubbles
That do last but a short minute.

Fame is but a moment
Fleeting fast away.
Beauty is like moonlight
Fading with the day.

Happiness is fragile
It can be broken by one word
Many people crying
But their voices never heard.

Hate, fear, and war
Hearts frozen to the core.
Tears and blood run together
Their stains will last forever.

Is there a purpose to the pain?
Something more than personal gain?
What are we all looking for?
Is there more beyond death's door?

Hearts are empty, eyes are full.
Death seems kind for life is cruel.
Running seems the only escape
From life's lonely dreary fate.

The confusion and sadness
The cruelty and shame
Oh how glad I am
I need not live this life again.

The Other Side of Heaven

It's the end of the world
They're screaming in fear
You're trying to find me
But I'm nowhere near.

Lover's sentiments whisper
Echoing on the breeze
Caressing a world fallen
Then everyone sees

The other side of heaven
Marching in on black cloud
Claiming lives of those who love
Wrapping them in cold shroud.

The other side of heaven
Is a dark and dismal place
Inhabitants devoid of feeling
Belief in love a hollow waste.

I watch from a distance
Betrayer of my own kind

Minion of the other side of heaven
Knowing love wasn't real to find.

I couldn't stay and hear
Last sweet lies fall from your lips.
Knew punishment was coming
For drinking love's poison sips.

My feelings have been uncertain
Even though you swore you cared
I thought it was a web of deciet
But maybe I was just scared.

Was it my disbelief in joy
That caused my world to fall?
My mis-trust of your love
That ruined love for all?

The broken lives around me
Result of my own empty heart.
My selfish fear of loving
Tore a world of love apart.

Ruler of the other side of heaven
With deep pain I realise
Disbelief and a place I created
Caused real loves demise.

My Last Day

Today I end a journey,
Shut a door behind me,
Leave my friends lonely,
Today is my last day.

Today I say goodbye,
Try in vain not to cry,
Take last looks with a sigh,
Today is my last day.

My time I have enjoyed here,
Don't want to leave, swallow fear,
Last goodbyes fall on my ear,
Today is my last day.

Faces I have grown to love,
12 years wasn't enough,
Life goes on with different stuff,
So today is my last day.

The clock ticks on so fast,
I can't bring back the past,
Memories will always last
From today, my last day.

Now I will be on my own,
Starting a life almost grown,
Picking flowers from seeds sown,
Tomorrow's my first day.

Goodbye Tonight

You left me at the party
I'm outside all alone
The footpath is my dancefloor
As I make my way home.

I'm barefoot moving freely
Touch the stars, I'm taking flight.
You made the world my party
When you said goodbye tonight.

So glad to be alone now
You've found another girl.
Relief makes me feel lighter
As I dance and sweep and twirl.

I've got a destination
Somewhere far from you.
I'm free to laugh and smile now
I'll dance into the blue.

Pirouette and kiss the morning
I party on past dawn.
Goodbye tonight and forever
Kick my heels and I'm gone.

The Island

My mother used to say
I was an island in the sea.
Now I'm drowning in the waves
That once protected me.

I can't breathe underwater
I'm reaching for a hand.
My fingers come back empty
Clutch ropes of dry sand.

Oceans of regret surrounding
Far from a friendly ear.
An island standing all alone
Beholden to rejection and fear.

Sorrow in the sunlight
Cutting beneath my waves
Standing strong and silently
It is solidarity that saves.

Needing none, trusting few
Replace flesh with cold stone
Treading depths of tortured mind
Heartbreak can never be shown.

An island am and always be
Pretense of independence strong.
Apppreance says I'm brave and well
So how could I say you're wrong?

For You

Hunger in my belly and a mouth full of breeze
I'd sell my soul for you down on my knees
A city of my flesh, every brick and stone
You're the salt in my wounds cut to the bone.

I need you, want you, hate you, and still
My spirit fights you and bends to your will.
Breath in my lungs but I can't breathe air
Fire in my eyes and a silent death stare.

Under your feet my future can be found
A handful of dirt plucked from the ground.
A heart in my chest now broken for you
The hearts in my hands are trembling too.

Sacrificed daily for pleasure and shame
Sweetness in thought though bitter in name
A thousand regrets claiming the throne
Question the crown usurping the known.

Sold on a promise and yet gifted a sting
Living for solace your answers may bring.
A slave and a solider, a pawn just to use
I'm yours all or nothing, to win or to lose.

www.ingramcontent.com/pod-product-compliance
Lightning Source LLC
LaVergne TN
LVHW021312200726
843509LV00012B/1877